Seasonings
winter

Seasonings
winter

daily devotions for changing times

DONNA L. HUISJEN

January through March

credo
house publishers

Seasonings: Winter
Daily Devotions for Changing Times

Copyright © 2012 by Donna Huisjen

Published in the United States by Credo House Publishers,
a division of Credo Communications, LLC, Grand Rapids, Michigan
www.credohousepublishers.com

ISBN: 978-1-935391-75-3

Scripture quotations taken from The Holy Bible,
New International Version® NIV®
Copyright © 1973, 1978, 1984, 2011 by Biblica, Inc.™
Used by permission. All rights reserved worldwide.

Cover and interior design: Sharon VanLoozenoord

First edition

winter

"Spring passes and one remembers one's innocence.
Summer passes and one remembers one's exuberance.
Autumn passes and one remembers one's reverence.
Winter passes and one remembers one's perseverance."

—Yoko Ono

"God's voice thunders in marvelous ways; he does great things beyond our understanding. He says to the snow, 'Fall on the earth,' and to the rain shower, 'Be a mighty downpour.' So that everyone he has made may know his work, he stops all people from their labor. The animals take cover; they remain in their dens. The tempest comes out from its chamber, the cold from the driving winds. The breath of God produces ice, and the broad waters become frozen."

(Job 37:5–10)

✻

"He sends his command to the earth; his word runs swiftly. He spreads the snow like wool and scatters the frost like ashes. He hurls down his hail like pebbles. Who can withstand his icy blast? He sends his word and melts them; he stirs up his breezes, and the waters flow."

(Psalm 147:15–18)

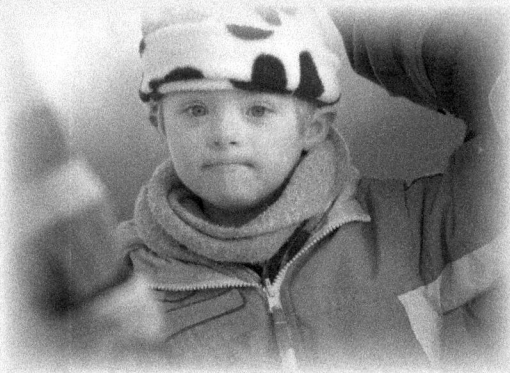

"*I* prefer winter and fall,
when you feel the bone structure
in the landscape—the loneliness
of it—the dead feeling of winter.
Something waits beneath it—the
whole story doesn't show."

—Andrew Wyeth

❋

January

"The cold was our pride,
the snow was our beauty.
It fell and fell, lacing day and
night together in a milky haze,
making everything quieter
as it fell, so that winter
seemed to partake of religion
in a way no other season did,
hushed, solemn."

—Patricia Hampl

January 1

Marking Time

*"And God said, 'Let there be lights
in the vault of the sky to separate
the day from the night, and let them
serve as signs to mark sacred times,
and days and years" (Genesis 1:14).*

God's marvelous creation marked the inception not only of organized matter but also of time. And with time came timekeepers—the sun, moon, and stars, governing the unfolding, circular march of the seasons. Nineteenth-century English essayist Charles Lamb commented that "No one ever regarded the First of January with indifference. It is that from which all date their time, and count upon what is left. It is the nativity of our common Adam."

As Christians, of course, we know both a different nativity and a different pivot point from which to mark our days—two of them, in fact, marked by Jesus' birth and resurrection. Make the most of the new year unfolding before you, reckoning "time" on the basis of its envelopment by eternity.

January 2

Numbered, Not Counted

"And even the very hairs of your head are all numbered" (Matthew 10:30).

For some reason I've always read this verse as though "numbered" were "counted." This may be one of those instances in which a knowledge of Greek would come in handy, but it occurs to me that these two verbs are nuanced differently. The idea of each of my hairs being so unique in God's sight as to have a particular identity (number) awes me even more than his keeping count of the total number that cling to my head at any given moment.

A related issue fits well with the beginning of a new year: God's faithful care and provision. Take a look at your hairbrush before you glibly toss that tangled clump of disengaged hairs into the wastebasket. What does this visual say to you as you ready yourself for the day . . . and for this dawning new year?

January 3

Post-Holiday Celebration

"Can you make the friends of the bridegroom fast while he is with them?"
(Luke 5:34).

The stretch between New Years Day and Easter can seem interminable. Not only have the year's closely compacted major holidays run their course, but many of us face unpunctuated routine in conjunction with harsh climatic conditions. Combine that with a daily round of usually late darkness early and early darkness later, and we can experience a postholiday jolt.

But who says we need to stop celebrating? That a nose-to-the-grindstone, belt-tightening stretch is called for to balance things out? With reference to Jesus' rhetorical question, above, no one can make us "fast" if our perspective doesn't call for it. Our bridegroom may no longer be with his Church in bodily form. But the reality is so much better as his Spirit indwells us in preparation for our celebration of his resurrection—the true high point of the year, of our individual lives, and of human history.

January 4

"Will There Be January?"

*"We declare God's wisdom, a mystery that
has been hidden and that God destined
for our glory before time began"
(1 Corinthians 2:7).*

"Granna, in the new world will there be
January?" I'll have to admit I was taken
slightly aback by the unexpected question.
In the verse above Paul reminds us that God
ordained his plan for human/salvation history before the beginning of the *time* that
defines our experience and understanding—
the same *time* that will wind down to its
close on the day of Christ's return. After that
. . . well, probably no January.

Wondering, as we all do, about the logis-
tics of life outside a time frame, I focus on
God's words through his prophet in Isaiah
65:17–18: "See, I will create new heavens
and a new earth. The former things will
not be remembered, nor will they come
to mind. But be glad and rejoice forever
in what I will create." I'm saddened to
think of giving up my memory—it's a part
of time, too, isn't it? Not to mention a vi-
tal "part" of the me I presently know. No,
Adelyn, there probably won't be a January.
But God's perfect love and wisdom, mani-
fested anew in what he will create, will infinitely exceed our need! Whatever he has
planned will be just right!

January 5

Your Place

"He brought me out into a spacious place;
he rescued me because he delighted in me"
(2 Samuel 22:20).

Yesterday's discussion of time leads me,
perhaps tangentially, to a consideration
of space or place. In one sense we as
Christians collectively inhabit a place so
roomy as to both transcend space and be
irrelevant to it. Because God's kingdom
permeates and infuses all space, filtering
into the darkest places on Earth, God's
people need to continuously push our
way into the darkness.

You've encountered the expression "a
sense of place." This has nothing to do
with confining concepts like location
either, reaching as it does into the more
subjective areas of belonging, well-being,
sanctuary, security, fitting or fitting in.
I hesitate mentioning sanctuary and security, because these words may con-
note erecting walls around ourselves. As
long as our modus operandi is to invite
and welcome others into our safe place,
though, this image is right on. Into what
spacious place has God brought you?

January 6

Belated Good News

"He spoke with great fervor and taught about Jesus accurately, though he knew only the baptism of John"
(Acts 18:25).

My granddaughter's exhilaration over a "coming" attraction isn't always real-time accurate. I chuckle (now in 2012) when she enthuses over the preview of a kid-enticing DVD "coming to theaters near you in spring 2006." Apollos, for all his exuberance about Jesus, suffered from a similar disconnect, though its topic was unrelated. Priscilla and Aquila took the misguided evangelist under their collective wing and updated him on Jesus' death, resurrection, and ascension.

Apollos recognized Israel's Messiah, putting his faith and hope in Jesus. How excited he must have been to get the rest of the story! There are millions still today who either haven't heard the Good News or lack the full picture. Who in your acquaintance could benefit from some enlightenment? What a difference it could make in their quality of life this year . . . and infinitely beyond!

January 7

Excess of Wonder?

"As soon as all the people saw Jesus,
they were overwhelmed with wonder"
(Mark 9:15).

People accustomed to isolation or familiar only with primitive surroundings have been known to go into a "shut-down" mode when confronted with more wonder than they can take in. Sadly, much of creation's grandeur is lost on us in the same way. Each of us encounters such a surfeit of the beautiful and awe inspiring that we tune out. Overstimulated, we become blind, unmoved, inobservant.

Jeannette Winterson (great name for this time of year, isn't it?) conveys this phenomenon in a different light: "They say that every snowflake is different. If that were true, how could the world go on? How could we ever get off our knees? How could we ever recover from the wonder of it?" I've always believed that bit of "trivia"—about the snowflakes, that is— for whatever it's worth. You too? They disappear, or accumulate so quickly I've never been able to tell . . .

January 8

Been There?

*"Have you entered the storehouses
of the snow?" (Job 38:22).*

We're unaccustomed to God's tone in
Job 38, which sounds to our ears—dare
I say it?—sarcastic and scathing. Listen to
the previous verse: "Surely you know, for
you were already born! You have lived
so many years!" Ouch! It isn't our job,
of course, to determine God's "right" to
be, do, or say anything. The Creator per-
sonifies goodness to the point that the
only thing he can't do is act contrary to
his nature. The whole premise of this
amazing book (one of my favorites) is
his love for faithful Job.

You and I haven't entered the storehouses
of the snow either, although we understand much more of scientific cause and
effect than Job did. But God continues to
reside on a plane infinitely higher than
our own. I, for one, benefit from a periodic reminder.

January 9

Standing Tall

"Epaphras . . . is always wrestling in prayer for you, that you may stand firm in all the will of God, mature and fully assured" (Colossians 4:12).

Dropping off Adelyn for kindergarten this morning, I watched her swish off in her snow pants for the playground, backpack thumping, hat slightly askew and anchored with "ear mugs." Ready to back out, I saw her fall and turn to gaze in my direction, question marks in her eyes: *Do I stand up and continue running or cry so Granna will comfort me?* Out of the corner of my eye I watched her come to a stand, throw one more resigned glance my way, and head toward the play equipment. It took discipline on both our parts to turn away.

Separating from our little ones isn't always easy, but it is a necessary step toward their maturation and independence. All of us fall in one way or another from time to time, and what a comfort to know that Jesus is there to catch us when we do. But in the regular course of things it's essential for each of us to stand on our own, firm and resolute within his will, mature and fully assured.

January 10

The Leveler

"Who knows what is good for a person in life, during the few and meaningless days they pass through like a shadow? Who can tell them what will happen under the sun after they are gone?"
(Ecclesiastes 6:12).

There's something pristine and exquisite about an untouched field of new-fallen snow, a picture of newness, the suggestion of a fresh, unsullied start. Tucked in its shared white blanket, everything looks crisp and united. The weed-choked yard flows seamlessly into the manicured plot next door. And the sun on the snow, or the moon on the snow, affords the darker world of winter a welcome 24/7 glow. Adrienne Ivey observes that "Everything is equal in the snow. . . . Everything looks clean and fresh and unmarred by time or use." But she moves on in an unexpected somber note: "Snow, like the silent death it counterfeits, is a great leveler."

We humans tend to be too much about status and distinction and curb appeal, too little about equality, unity, solidarity. Physical death will indeed be our leveler, but in the life to come we'll be clothed, one and all, in dazzling white robes. Status and distinction aren't good for us now, and they won't divide us then.

January 11

Preoccupied

"'Don't bother me. The door is already locked, and my children and I are in bed. I can't get up and give you anything'"
(Luke 11:7).

My youngest daughter, Khristina, Adelyn's single mom, not only works long hours but lives (at the time of this writing; the situation has been back and forth) forty miles from my condo and her job. Her uncertain schedule necessitates some unexpected sleepovers, and lacking a guest bed we three generations of "girls" crash together. Last night we were dropping off to sleep when the phone rang. Hearing the voice of Angie, my middle daughter, I interrupted in a whisper that no doubt sounded like a hiss: "Talk fast. I'm already in bed with Khris and Addie." In response to a mumbled "I'm afraid I have the wrong number," I realized I was addressing a stranger.

I chuckled at what must have been a disconcerting response for my unwary caller, and the verse above came unbidden to my mind. Unlike me, God is never indisposed or predisposed. And he doesn't mind late calls.

January 12

"Have Salt"

*"'Have salt among yourselves,
and be at peace with each other'"
(Mark 9:50).*

Seasoning, whether salt or any other, adds that zing that piques our taste buds and draws us back for more. Without it, life would be bland indeed. Variety is the spice of life—so goes the old adage—and that certainly applies to the mix of human beings on the planet and in our lives. The credit, of course, goes to the infinitely inventive Creator, but we're wise to do what we can to foster it.

Perhaps if we were less competitive in our relationships, we would have more of the peace of which Jesus speaks. Products as we are of the Master Artist, we have no need to replicate anyone else. If you're married, what particular zest does your spouse bring to your union? Single or married, what traits and abilities make you special? If you're a member of a church family, do you relish one another's company and unique contributions? What does Jesus' injunction to "Have salt among yourselves" say to you personally?

January 13

A Particular Grace

"Out of his fullness we have all received
grace in place of grace already given"
(John 1:16).

Seated alone this morning in a busy diner
sipping coffee between errands, I appre-
ciated the surge of life around me. Just as
an elderly man shambled by sporting a
jacket touting the Saladin Shrine Clown
Unit, I overheard a snatch of conversation
from two men at a nearby table, including
"You have to have a particular grace, given
to you by God, to be able to withstand
that." I'm not sure what "that" was or
is, but it occurred to me that individuals
have their own unique ways of confront-
ing and enduring—and helping others
confront and endure—hard times.

John's words, above, speak of grace piled
atop grace, perhaps alluding to the special
measure of which the articulate stranger
in the restaurant was speaking. God is indeed indulgent with that commodity,
dispensing grace a la mode when his children need it. How much more precious to
the hurting than any amount of feel-good
clowning around or other distractions!

January 14

Foundation

"He will be the sure foundation for your times" (Isaiah 33:6).

Our times indeed cry out for a sure foundation, and God's Word assures us that we have one. In Job 38:4 God asks rhetorically, "Where were you when I laid the earth's foundation?" And Zechariah 12:1 refers to the "Lord, who stretches out the heavens, who lays the foundation of the earth."

But above that immovable subfloor is the individual foundation for each of our lives. That one isn't always so steady—nor perhaps should it be, benefiting as we do from periodic wake-up calls and grounding checks. "It's a good thing to have all the props pulled out from under us occasionally," observes Madeleine L'Engle. "It gives us some sense of what is rock under our feet, and what is sand." "Nevertheless," asserts Paul (that's one of his favorite words), "God's solid foundation stands firm, sealed with this inscription: 'The Lord knows those who are his'" (2 Timothy 2:19). What a blessed underpinning for times like these!

January 15

Position

*"'And who knows but that you
have come to your royal position
for such a time as this?'"*
(Esther 4:14).

"I can't get to sleep, Granna."

"Just go back to bed and find another position."

"It's the only position I have!"

I suppose that's true for a five-year-old. But human standings do change. Some of us, like Esther, might even rise to a high position from which we're uniquely equipped to serve the kingdom. Yet from a spiritual perspective each of us approaches our Lord with identical status. Having divested ourselves of any perceived merit that might have distinguished us, we stand before him in humble submission and overflowing gratitude. It's the only position we have—and what a privileged one!

January 16

Anchored

*"We have this hope as an anchor
for the soul, firm and secure"
(Hebrews 6:19).*

"Too many people," observed James F.
Byrnes, "are thinking of security instead
of opportunity. They seem more afraid
of life than death." The case could just as
well be made, I suppose, for humanity's
frantic quest for security being an effort to
stave off that worst-case scenario, but the
fact remains that fears about tomorrow
(the awake-and-aware tomorrow) are a
huge behavioral driver.

It shouldn't be that way with us. We of all
people can—yes, and must (if we want to
avoid hurting the sensitive Spirit!)—face
life as those who are anchored, firm and
secure. That stance in itself goes a long
way toward promoting Christ's cause.
Those around us who sense themselves
to be "at sea," agitated by the currents and
entangled in flotsam, will notice and desire the mooring we enjoy.

January 17

Evermore

*"We always carry around in our body
the death of Jesus, so that the life of
Jesus may also be revealed in our body"
(2 Corinthians 4:10).*

Paul makes it clear that Jesus' followers
will suffer in his name. There's no might
about it. And that isn't a bad thing. In
fact, it affirms our connection with Christ
and authenticates our witness.

What the world doesn't get is how we can
embrace suffering. Without being dour
masochists, that is. Could what we have
to gain really be so fabulous that we're
willing to lose everything else in the process? That kind of ultimate eludes a grasp-
ing world, whose mantra seems to be
more, more, more! Perhaps the difference
can be condensed into one space: are we
looking for ever more or for evermore?
The world needs to see through our words
and actions that it can't be both ways.

January 18

Doldrums

"You, LORD, keep my lamp burning;
my God turns my darkness into light"
(Psalm 18:28).

Natural light is so essential to the human psyche that some people need special lamps to simulate it during the bleak months. Have you noticed the differences in literature and culture between, say, the English and the Spanish? Generalities can be risky, but I picture those subjected on a regular basis to London fog having a heavier tread and rounder shoulders than those who bask in sunlight, savoring equally their fiestas and siestas. My ancestors, the Dutch, a contemplative bunch, likely gravitated to gray West Michigan on the basis of familiarity.

If you're someone for whom darkness brings doldrums, don't be too hard on yourself. Take advantage of what light you can—inviting its presence both physically and spiritually. "For God, who said, 'Let light shine out of darkness,' made his light shine in our hearts to give us the light of the knowledge of God's glory displayed in the face of Christ" (2 Corinthians 4:6). Wow! That deserves two or three readings!

January 19

Creation Birthed

"'From whose womb comes the ice?
Who gives birth to the frost from the
heavens?'" (Job 38:29).

During one of those transitional half
hours rapidly cycling from rain to sleet
to snow I made the rather inane comment, "There's something in the air, and
it isn't exactly snow." Adelyn prompted
helpfully from her booster seat behind
me, "Maybe God?"

The lovely image from the book of Job,
above, comes directly from God's mouth,
making the questions seem all the more
rhetorical. I've never thought in terms
of God *birthing* ice, frost, or snow, but
I can't imagine a more intimate image of
the relationship between Creator and created. If God cares that much for every icy
droplet, how much more does he yearn
for fellowship with you and me?

January 20

"More Than These?"

"'Simon, son of John, do you love me more than these?'" (John 21:15).

Overheard from the next room: "Mommy, I love you forty-ninety-ninety-ninety-ninety-ninety times. How much do you love me?" That's it, the question that drives humanity. It's first "heard" in the searching gaze of the newborn, trained on her mother's soon-to-be-memorized features. And it continues to be asked in one form or another through the duration of her life.

Once we know our heavenly Father, the dynamic is repeated. "How much do you love me?" we challenge him. And Jesus, our Savior and Lord, asks the same of us, as he once did Peter. That universal question, coming from either direction, demands the answer of infinity. How much indeed do we love Jesus? More than *these*? (You fill in the antecedent.)

January 21

Tuesdays

" . . . to those sanctified in Christ Jesus
and called to be his holy people, together
with all those everywhere who call on the
name of our Lord Jesus Christ"
(1 Corinthians 1:2).

All of life is sacred. Sunday mornings. Tuesday afternoons. Worship services. Marketing meetings. Saturday late-nights. True, the New Testament refers to holy people, not so much to holy times, places, or things. But it's my belief that we as believers have a sort of Midas touch, transforming whatever we contact into wholesomeness and clarity. Because our "hands [and hearts] have touched" (1 John 1:1) our Lord Jesus Christ, and we've come away different.

Led by the Spirit, we're no longer inclined to evil. But neither are we a shoe-in for choosing the good in a given situation. For us as Christ's ambassadors, all of life needs to be handled with deliberate care. In the words of Abraham Joshua Heschel, "Our concern is not how to worship in the catacombs, but how to remain human in the skyscrapers." That's a good challenge, especially for those Tuesday afternoons after a busy weekend.

January 22

Whose?

"Whether we live or die, we belong
to the Lord" (Romans 14:8).

Ruth Stout has observed that "In spring, summer and fall people sort of have an open season on each other; only in winter, in the country, can you have longer, quiet stretches when you can savor belonging to yourself." I too relish the relative isolation of the cold months.

Yet we as Christians have no illusions of belonging to ourselves; Paul had it exactly right, above. But barely two chapters earlier the apostle had referred to a different kind of belonging: "In Christ we, though many, form one body, and each member belongs to all the others" (Romans 12:5). Far from having an open season on one another, I think as I gaze at a bundled neighbor hurrying toward his car, when the conditions outdoors become conducive we can regularly season each other's days with caring and communication. It takes a little more effort to do so in the cold, I remind myself, but the need is no less real.

Synonyms

*"God is love. Whoever lives in love
lives in God, and God in them"
(1 John 4:16).*

Canadian poet and novelist Margaret
Atwood commented that "The eskimos
had fifty-two names for snow because it
was important to them." Her conclusion:
"there ought to be as many for love." The
English language is precise, with a wealth
of finely nuanced synonyms and near
synonyms. And yet we'd be hard-pressed
to come up with fifty-plus nouns meaning love.

We as Christians are to be defined by love
in a more intrinsic and inclusive sense
than an Inuit is defined by snow. But our
culture is profoundly confused about
love, too often mistaking it for lust, infat-
uation, or possession. Hardly nuanced or
subtle, those often fleeting passions need
no synonyms. How important is Christian
love—the real thing—in your life?

January 24

Delight

"If you call the Sabbath a delight . . .
then you will find your joy in the LORD"
(Isaiah 58:13–14).

As an editor and writer I appreciate
this quote from William Safire: "Only
in grammar can you be more than perfect." I'm convinced, though, that there
are other areas in which we can be hap-
pily and effectively less than compliant—
a lesson my parents taught me, twice that
I can immediately recall, when I was six
or seven. First they squirreled me out
of the hospital in a wheelchair during a
month-long stay to visit my siblings on
the grass; and, second, my mom and aunt
defied our 1950s church's taboo by bring-
ing their collective broods to *Bambi*. Dad
repeated the lesson several years later,
when as a young widower he took us kids
out to dinner one Sunday morning after
church.

Jesus, as we know, was all about the spirit
of the law. My concern is that our temptation is to ignore both its letter and its
spirit. Today as always, keeping the Sabbath a delight requires thoughtful, inten-
tional balance.

January 25

Your Healer

"I am the LORD, who heals you"
(Exodus 15:26).

The buffer of some five years separates
me from a series of hard memories—
memories I seem to have wrapped in silk
like a fly in a spider's web, intending never
to reopen. For a while I avoided writing
about the "loss" of three beloved grandchildren to out-of-state adoption, afraid
of sounding melodramatic. Now I find
it hard at times to dredge up these rec-
ollections even in my own mind. But
I've decided I would be less than honest avoiding a subject with which others
might resonate.

I have no idea where you are in the in-
fancy of this year. What I do know is that
life's highlights presuppose lowlights
and periods of darkness. But the incredible news is that it gets easier. Your hurt
may be more profound than my hopefully
temporary loss, but God is present in your
anguish, weeping with you as he did at
Lazarus's grave. "I am the LORD," he in-
tones tenderly, "who heals you."

January 26

Namesake

*"I bear your name, L*ord *God Almighty"*
(Jeremiah 15:16).

Bearing God's name means that each of us as a believer is his namesake—and more. Throughout the Old Testament we find instances of God's Name being synonymous with his Presence. In that sense bearing his name—being directly identified with him—has an almost tangible quality, going far beyond representing him symbolically.

The Old Testament refers not only to God's namesake but to his "name's sake" (Psalm 23:3). Like it or not, the way we conduct ourselves in this world reflects directly on the name and reputation of the One we serve. The world knows exactly who we are—and assesses him accordingly. "That isn't fair!" we may want to protest. It might be beneficial at that point for us to step back and ask a question: unfair for us—or for him?

January 27

Bottled Up

"You have collected all my tears in your bottle" (Psalm 56:8 NLT).

I don't cry often, but when I do I can be powerless to stanch the flow. It comforts me to think of God lovingly collecting those liquid symbols of helplessness, injustice, or despair. Somehow picturing a little vial of "holy water" with my name on it makes a painful memory seem to matter.

One day God will right all wrongs, including those, profound or trivial, that have affected your and my lives. I wonder whether he'll pour out my vial then; in that renewed garden those old owies and injustices will have lost their relevance. What I do know for sure is that "The Sovereign LORD will wipe away [any residual] tears from all faces" (Isaiah 25:8). What an achingly poignant image!

January 28

Stepping Out in the Spirit

*"Brothers and sisters, choose seven men
from among you who are known
to be full of the Spirit and wisdom"
(Acts 6:3).*

I'm mildly amused by an expression
used to describe appearances in public
(as opposed to scheduled public appearances) by female celebrities. A head-
turning headline might be something like
"_____ steps out in a department-store
frock." The observation typically applies
to a younger celebrity, and the implication
is usually a lapse in fashion judgment.

While in one sense we can't assess the
spiritual condition of another person,
we can be pretty sure that an individual who not only claims to be a Christian but exudes the Spirit of Christ is the
real deal. When we step out in the Spirit
we too should turn heads. And that head-
turning opens the door for the Spirit to
turn hearts!

January 29

Cut Off

"Do your best to get here before winter"
(2 Timothy 4:21).

Paul's cryptic request to Timothy, above, has a winsome quality. Languishing in a prison cell in Rome without so much as his cloak for comfort, the apostle battled cold, isolation, and a feeling of abandonment. Reliving the harrowing, late-autumn voyage and shipwreck of a few years earlier, he no doubt also feared for the safety of his trusted friend and son in the faith.

With its icy fingers, skeletal branches, and gray sky, winter is for many the inhospitable season. For those wintering alone it can be cruel, heartless, unrelenting. We set travel plans and dates contingent on conditions; "weather permitting" hangs over our best-laid plans. For whose (human) company do you long while in the grip of winter? What steps can you take to reach out even when you feel like curling up inside yourself? If you suspect that others are experiencing this kind of seclusion, what can you do, before and during the winter months, to alleviate their desolation?

January 30

Back . . . or Forth?

"If I forget you, Jerusalem, may my right hand forget its skill. May my tongue cling to the roof of my mouth if I do not remember you, if I do not consider Jerusalem my highest joy" (Psalm 137:5–6).

The raw grief of God's people in Babylon makes this psalm poignant. Picture the scene as the exiles are forced to hang their harps from the poplars to entertain their jeering captors with "one of the songs of Zion." And yet God didn't want his people to wring their hands and dwell on the past, instructing them through Jeremiah to "seek the peace and prosperity of the city to which I have carried you into exile. Pray to the LORD for it, because if it prospers, you too will prosper" (Jeremiah 29:7).

Margaret Fairless Barger says of nostalgia, "To look backward for a while is to refresh the eye, to restore it, and to render it the more fit for its prime function of looking forward." I find my aging self more prone to reminisce. From an earthly perspective, there's more to capture my imagination behind me than before. If I only knew a tad more of my eternal future, I wonder where my focus would be.

January 31

Miscues

"'This can be nothing but sadness of heart'"
(Nehemiah 2:2).

Ever notice how tightly you walk in the wintertime—head retracted inside your collar, muscles flexed and steeled against the cold, and footsteps mincing for fear of a black ice encounter? You are, and look, intent on your destination and less than eager for an interruption.

"Every man has his secret sorrows which the world knows not," observed poet Henry Wadsworth Longfellow, "and often-times we call a man cold when he is only sad." Sad people, like those efficient winter walkers, don't saunter. They trudge. And their gait and demeanor easily peg them as forbidding, dour, ice encased. There are variations on the theme. When have you misinterpreted a shy person as arrogant or a self-conscious individual as standoffish? We owe it to one another to offer the benefit of the doubt. We might end up avoiding a future close friend just waiting to be discovered. At the very least we might offer a ray of sunshine to another someone for whom Christ deeply cares.

February

"Winter, which strips
the leaves from around us,
makes us see the distant regions
they formerly concealed; so does
old age rob us of our enjoyments,
only to enlarge the prospect
of eternity before us."

—Jean Paul Richter

February 1

The Essential Dynamic

"What do you have that you did not receive? And if you did receive it, why do you boast as though you did not?"
(1 Corinthians 4:7).

I doubt anyone will disagree with this sentiment from Franklin Thomas: "One day our descendants will think it incredible that we paid so much attention to things like the amount of melanin in our skin or the shape of our eyes or our gender instead of the unique identities of each of us as complex human beings." But is this coming regret a fact?

Unregenerate human nature doesn't progress. That's true, but it overlooks the central dynamic of authentic change. In Paul's words, "Those who live in accordance with the Spirit have their minds set on what the Spirit desires" (Romans 8:5). If an honest self-assessment reveals traces of racism, sexism, or self-pride, ask the Spirit at the commencement of this black history month to revise your attitude and revive your resolve. His presence is the one change agent that works!

February 2

"I Am He"

"Even to your old age and gray hairs
I am he, I am he who will sustain you.
I have made you and I will carry you"
(Isaiah 46:4).

Which is the more astonishing: God's creating or his carrying (you, that is; let's make it personal)? Jeremy Taylor thought this through and placed the two on a par: "To preserve a man alive in the midst of so many chances and hostilities, is as great a miracle as to create him."

Your and my Abba is the doting kind, the kind who is only too happy to heft our frail bodies at both ends of our human life cycle—and in between "as needed." My tradition calls this preservation providence, but the reality transcends any label. Our Creator/Provider declares himself in no uncertain terms: "I am he"! And what a comfort to know that I'm his!

Limits?

*"Do not gloat when your enemy falls;
when they stumble, do not let your heart
rejoice, or the LORD will see and disapprove
and turn his wrath away from them"*
(Proverbs 24:17–18).

Realization of the extent of God's love for all people can be jarring—and unwelcome, as it was for Jonah. The inescapable reality is that God is actively involved with and concerned for all of humanity, including those who will not come to salvation.

To what extent are we, Christ's followers, prepared to follow suit? Where do we draw our line in the sand when it comes to tolerating injustice—and (a more dangerous question) its proponents? The referents may have been different, but Eleanor Roosevelt asked a question years ago that needs to prick us still: "When will our consciences grow so tender that we will act to prevent human misery rather than avenge it?" The implications are global, but also personal and individual. Who have you written off as God's enemy, unworthy of Christ's love? Might it not be prudent to make sure *he* has?

February 4

Evergreen

"This calls for patient endurance on the part of the people of God who keep his commands and remain faithful to Jesus" (Revelation 14:12).

Adelyn and I were admiring the bolded white outlines showcasing the skeletal bone structures of snow-encased trees. But her gaze took in more than mine: "Granna, I like the snow best on the everlasting trees." No, evergreens won't live forever (at least not during this dispensation), but barring natural disaster, disease, infestation, or human intervention most trees do enjoy a significant lifespan. And while they live they serve as models of the best approach to life; in the words of Antoine de Saint-Exupéry, "The tree is a slow, enduring force straining to win the sky."

You and I, in contrast, will be around not for the duration (there won't be one) but forever. As children and heirs of our eternal Creator and God, we were conceived and born everlasting. We owe it to our Master to be evergreen—fertile, fruitful, and productive—in his name. And that kind of faithfulness requires of us the same stalwart perseverance as a tree.

February 5

The Long View

*"With fire and with his sword the L*ORD
will execute judgment on all people"
(Isaiah 66:16).

"True peace is not merely the absence of
tension," noted Dr. Martin Luther King
Jr., going on, "it is the presence of justice." Adelyn and I are in the habit of end-
ing our nighttime ritual with an exchange
of "Peace, be still." Jesus' words act as a
tonic; swathed in well-being, Addie's eye-
lids flutter to a close. Life's storms indeed generate tension, but the peace of
Christ has an "all's right with the world"
dimension that's irresistible to us fairness-
craving humans.

We'd be naïve to suggest that it's all right
yet, although Isaiah 65 reminds us that
it will be. The prophet moves on, above,
to remind us that God's nature demands
justice—that things will get worse before
they get perfect. But we can take incredible comfort in the long view God has
opened for us. "Be still," our Lord calls
out, "and know that I am God" (Psalm
46:10). Indeed, "be still before the LORD,
all mankind" (Zechariah 2:13).

February 6

Faith in the Narrows

*"The angel of the Lord moved on
ahead and stood in a narrow place
where there was no room to turn"
(Numbers 22:26).*

You know the story: the prophet bribed
to curse Israel was stopped by an unseen
angel blocking the narrow mountain pass.
Unseen, that is, except by the frantic donkey, which takes the only sensible course
of action and, despite beatings, lies down.
In lieu of *"heehaw!"* the valiant "steed"
asks rhetorically, "Have I been in the
habit of doing this to you?" The upshot:
Balaam sees the angel and follows its instructions to speak only God's words.

We've all been there, between that rock
and that hard place. What's your charac-
teristic response? Rage? Obstinate blindness? Beating your donkey? "Life without
faith . . . ," observed George Lancaster
Spalding, "is too narrow a space to live."

February 7

Heart to Heart

*"The LORD would speak to Moses
face to face, as one speaks to a friend"
(Exodus 33:11).*

It isn't just that close friends talk face-to-face. What's important is their uncanny ability to speak heart to heart. It's that "telepathy," that unwavering empathy that can speak volumes, with or without words. I'm amazed at the example of Job's friends, sitting for a week in imperturbable silence, simply sharing the load of grief. "Sorrow," so goes an African proverb, "is like a precious treasure, shown only to friends."

Whether or not we recognize it, God is that kind of friend. Have you ever thought of prayer as a continuous, unbroken stream, at times dipping below consciousness, only to resurface in occasional verbal communication? As the quiet camaraderie of two who are so in tune that words become superfluous? That kind of prayer needs no "over and out." Its "Amen," rather than a signal of termination, serves as a periodic assent, a heartfelt interjection of "So let it be!"

February 8

Balance

*"It is good to grasp the one and
not let go of the other. Whoever fears
God will avoid all extremes"
(Ecclesiastes 7:18).*

God is a God of balance. Which isn't to
say he's looking for apathetic or lackadai-
sical followers. Still, walking in the middle of the road (that narrow path to life)
is a good idea. "Extremes," voiced George
Chapman, "though contrary, have the like
effects. Extreme heat kills, and so extreme
cold." Extremes can also bring about extreme reactions in different directions. I've
known a father who raised his kids in an
atmosphere of religious extremism, a dad
who lost one to a virtual shutdown and
another to rebellion.

God is a God of balance. Between justice
and mercy, wrath and love, sovereignty
and the endowment of free will, transcen-
dence and intimacy, divinity and the taking on of flesh. He's intimately involved
with the Church, Christ's bride; his Spirit
continuously works within her to main-
tain balance in diversity.

February 9

A Unique Approach

*"Suddenly a light from heaven
flashed around him. He fell to the ground
and heard a voice say to him, 'Saul, Saul,
why do you persecute me?'"*
(Acts 9:3–4).

I've come across some dramatic accounts
of God interrupting the lives of Middle-
Eastern Muslims in an up-front man-
ner that instilled in me a twinge of envy.
These were descriptions of extraordinary,
face-to-face (dare I say "in your face"?)
confrontations in which God literally en-
veloped people with his love, introducing
himself as their Father—a concept abso-
lutely new to them.

Beyond wishing that God might be a tad
less subtle in his approaches to the rest
of us, I'm awed and comforted by these
manifestations of his power and sovereignty. One way or another, we can rest
assured that his modus operandi with
each of us will be just right.

February 10

Eclipse

*"He has rescued us from the dominion
of darkness and brought us into
the kingdom of the Son he loves"
(Colossians 1:13).*

Both the dark domain and the kingdom
of light permeate the New Testament and
our world, the one seeking to promote
and the other to expel the blackness of sin
and its consequences. Their interplay is
seen and felt continuously, each seeking
to impinge upon the other with stabbing
point and counterpoint.

We as Christians, though, too often fail
to recognize the mismatch between the
two in terms of power and permanence.
If we would only be bolder to claim and
acclaim the superiority of our side, we
would sense the darkness beating a hasty
retreat. I like this analogy from Beverly
Sills: "Christians should never fail to
sense the operation of an angelic glory.
It forever eclipses the world of demonic
powers, as the sun does a candle's light."

February 11

Covered

*"David says . . . when he speaks
of the blessedness of the one to whom God
credits righteousness apart from works:
'Blessed are those whose transgressions
are forgiven, whose sins are covered'"*
(Romans 4:6–7).

I like the analogy of "covered" sins. The idea isn't of a cover-up or concealment but of a cancelling out or disappearance. Our cleansed heart is a blank screen, not a repainted wall or retouched photo. The reality of our status, though, doesn't necessarily impinge on our understanding or acceptance of our position in God's sight.

It's you and I, not God, who won't let go of sin's residue. You and I who continue to tote around its memory, hoping its no-longer-existent ugliness won't show through. Ironically, I suspect it may be my sinful pride that keeps the memories alive—my ego-driven desire to cover myself. But thanks be to God: that tendency too has been covered.

February 12

Direct Line

"The throne of God and of the Lamb will be in the city, and his servants will serve him. They will see his face" (Revelation 22:3–4).

When it comes to technology, Khristina is the work-around queen extraordinaire. Alongside my television stands a tower of machines, with an Amazonian maze of chords looping to the floor behind it. Not having touched a DVD for some time, I attempted to play one recently. Avoiding both of the nonworking DVD players, I slotted the disk into the second-to-the-top gaming device but was stumped from there. A call to Khris at work yielded the instruction to "play with it." (I now know—not through playing but by explicit instruction—I have to switch out the three color-coded wires leading to the TV [if the topmost gaming device has been in use]; set the TV to AV2; and at the "play" prompt hit X on the airplane-steering-wheel-shaped controller for the second gaming device.)

All of which reminds me of the hoops through which God's Old Testament people had to jump to gain access to God. Not so for us. No complicated hookups, no intermediaries, no baffling instructions! Through Christ we share direct "access to the Father by one Spirit" (Ephesians 2:18). Hallelujah!

February 13

Access

"The Lord is close to the brokenhearted
and saves those who are crushed in spirit"
(Psalm 34:18).

An intensely private person, poet Emily
Dickinson refused to let her doctor exam-
ine her. Word has it she insisted on pass-
ing by the doorway of the room where
the doctor sat, expecting him to analyze
her kidney condition by a fleeting glimpse
of her fully clothed body.

An unknown author has it that "God can
heal a broken heart, but He has to have
all the pieces." No doubt he could appropriate the pieces we try to withhold, could
wrest or wrangle away from us whatever
it is we want to conceal. But a coerced
wholeness would do us no good. Intimacy with God, and consequent healing,
won't happen for us if we're willing to do
no more than stroll past his doorway.

February 14

Your Song of Songs

"Many waters cannot quench love;
rivers cannot sweep it away"
(Song of Songs 8:7).

The picture I get from these words is of trying to dilute the strength of love by overwhelming it with deterrents (that isn't detergents). But love, like the God who embodies it, is indestructible.

What thoughts on love does Valentine's Day raise for you? The nature of the holiday suggests a focus on romantic as does the Song of Songs. This remarkable book of the Bible makes no apology for celebrating the shared physical, sensuous bond between spouses. As long as you're living within his will, appreciate and enjoy this facet of love. Focusing on your loved one, use this day (or night) as an opportunity to sing together your own unique "song of songs."

February 15

The Stretch

"We also glory in our sufferings, because we know that suffering produces perseverance; perseverance, character; and character, hope"
(Romans 5:3–4).

These two short verses remind me of February. "Come again!" you may say. It might be a stretch to equate February with suffering, but if you've grown weary of gradations of gray you'll relate to the association. Biding our time in the bleak midwinter bolsters our patience and toughens our resolve—or at least our resignation. Tolerating winter produces perseverance.

What about character? Well, in the words of Gail Barison, "From winter we learn silence and acceptance and the stillness thickens." Moving right along to hope is a no-brainer. If any single season is conducive to anticipation, it's the approach to spring—far away as this transition might seem more than a month from its official debut, which tends to run ahead, here in West Michigan, of its climatic presentation. More significantly, we're within sight of Lent and its glorious culmination on Resurrection Sunday. If it seems a stretch to flex that enthusiasm right now, let's rely on our newly enhanced character to produce the requisite hope. It won't be all that long now.

February 16

Before and After

"Before the coming of this faith, we were held in custody under the law"
(Galatians 3:23).

Enforced obedience is never a sign of maturity. Whether the custody language Paul uses here is associated with adolescence or incarceration, the upshot is the same: life lived under law or rules is necessary for the juvenile and the socially irresponsible.

Paul's distinction has to do with the cycle not of human life but of redemption history. Gone are the days of slavish obedience to hard and fast rules. "In" is the liberation of a voluntary obedience (unforced, not enforced), based on love and gratitude for salvation. What more meaningful motivators, not for compliance alone but for deeds of nobility and generosity?

February 17

Out-Loving Verbal Sin

*"Even my close friend, someone I trusted,
one who shared my bread, has turned
against me" (Psalm 41:9).*

The practical fallout from specific sins can
affect us far beyond the forgiveness stage.
As expressed by Friedrich Nietzsche, "I'm
not upset that you lied to me. I'm upset
that from now on I can't believe you."

Gossip and verbal betrayal of trust can be
notoriously hard to outlive—and to out-
love. Such sins may stretch trust to the
breaking point and beyond, and the rift
can be permanent. I'm thankful that it
isn't that way with God, and I pray that
he'll curb my own tendency to hurt others
verbally. At the same time I seek, with his
help, to increase my elasticity in dealing
with those who have wronged me.

February 18

Unseen Growth

"The gospel is bearing fruit and growing throughout the whole world—just as it has been doing among you since the day you heard it and truly understood God's grace" (Colossians 1:6).

February may present as the stagnant month, but beneath the ground and within the gnarled branches frenetic activity is taking place. God's modus operandi in the natural world carries over to his work in human hearts. Poet William Cullen Bryant remarked that the "February sunshine steeps your boughs and tints the buds and swells the leaves within."

I'm not sure of the seasonal connection, but the Spirit—that "shy" member of the Trinity—performs his sanctifying work beneath the surface, transforming, tweaking, and honing before we can burst into bloom in fruitful service. The same is true on the mission field, where unspectacular years may culminate in a blazing increase. The growth of faith within the world and in our hearts is steady, despite what we see as spurts and surges. If you're uneasy about the growth rate in yourself or others, leave that angst with the Spirit; he takes no vacations.

February 19

Fullness of Glory

"Praise be to his glorious name forever;
may the whole earth be filled with his glory"
(Psalm 72:19).

William Shakespeare expressed a pessimistic view of human celebrity, stating that "glory is like a circle in the water, which never ceaseth to enlarge itself, till by broad spreading it disperse to naught." We all know how easily noteworthiness can degenerate in our fickle world to notoriety, fame to infamy, and following to forgetfulness.

As Solomon reminds us, above, God's glory is different altogether, increasing exponentially as his renown spreads throughout the world. And his glory is anything but novel, trendy, or fleeting; its staying power through generations and millennia begins for us to define "forever." Unbeknownst to most of its inhabitants, this earth looks forward to that day when it "will be filled with the knowledge of the Lord as the waters cover the sea" (Isaiah 11:9). Filled too with his glory!

Bitter

*"'Call me Mara, because the Almighty
has made my life very bitter. I went
away full, but the LORD has brought
me back empty. Why call me Naomi?'"
(Ruth 1:20–21).*

The name Marah (bitter) has come up
before in Old Testament history: a des-
ert spring with acrid water earned itself
that name when the disgruntled Israelites railed against Moses there (Exodus
15:23). A sour, resentful attitude strikes
us as ungrateful and un-Christian. And it
does nothing for the social status of the
person giving in to it.

It's interesting to me, though, that in neither of these accounts does God punish
negativity or sulkiness. Naomi finds her
empty arms filled with a grandson who
will become the great-grandfather of David
and a forebear of Jesus. And God leads the
Israelites on to a refreshing oasis. Is it just
possible that God is more gracious in this
regard than we are? Next time I'm frus-
trated by someone else's pessimism, I need
to pray for the ability both to withstand
and to understand. Bitterness can morph
into a way of life, but it's possible with a
sensitive touch to nip it in the bud.

February 21

Every Intricacy

"Out of the north he comes in golden splendor; God comes in awesome majesty"
(Job 37:22).

Scottish poet William Sharp captures for me much of winter's tranquil beauty in the following snapshot: "There is nothing in the world more beautiful than the forest clothed to its very hollows in snow. It is the still ecstasy of nature, wherein every spray, every blade of grass, every spire of reed, every intricacy of twig, is clad with radiance."

Winter specializes in close-ups. From beads of water dangling uniformly from berries to the tinkling wonder of ice-encased branches to the steady drip of sun-touched icicles to filigreed snow-flakes to telltale tracks across an otherwise mirror-smooth snow pack, winter's detailed wonders favor contemplation. And yet its unbroken vistas can soothe and satisfy the most farsighted soul. If you're by nature a winter appreciator, enjoy the waning season. If you're eager for spring, it isn't too late to retrain your eyes and heart to respond to February's own brand of golden splendor and awesome majesty.

February 22

Mountain Mettle

*"The Sovereign L*ORD* is my strength;*
he makes my feet like the feet of a deer,
he enables me to tread on the heights"
(Habakkuk 3:19).

Billy Graham chose a different image, but his picture of life on the precipice is similar: "As Christians face storms of adversity, they may rise with more beauty. They are like trees that grow on mountain ridges— battered by winds, yet trees in which we find the strongest wood."

We've all felt ourselves perched above a sheer cliff face, assaulted by the relentless forces of circumstance and evil. The ground gave way before my feet five years ago with the loss of three grandchildren— then ages four, five, and six—to out-of-state adoption . . . and, I pray, a better life, though I have no means of verification. Amazingly, or perhaps not so amazingly for me as a Christian, the Lord blessed me that day with a toehold. And it wasn't long before I recognized that my position on that mountainside was that much closer to him.

Dis-courage-ment

*"David also said to Solomon his son,
'Be strong and courageous, and do the work.
Do not be afraid or discouraged, for the LORD
God, my God, is with you. He will not fail
you or forsake you until all the work for the
service of the temple of the LORD is finished'"*
(1 Chronicles 28:20).

Multiple generations share the experience
of having learned the power of "I think
I can" from a delightful children's story.
Whether it's a matter of mind over matter or the exercise of psyching ourselves
up, we've all experienced the importance
of mental preparation for accomplish-
ing a difficult task. "Discouragement,"
pointed out an unknown author, "is not
the absence of adequacy but the absence
of courage."

To a certain degree we'll find ourselves
as adequate as we think we are, provided
our self-assessment is realistic. But we as
Christians have the unspeakable advantage of drawing upon an unlimited power
source. If it's a task God wants us to do
(and this goes beyond obvious kingdom
work), we share with David and Solomon
the certainty of a more than adequate in-
fusion of God's strength.

February 24

Progression

"You are no longer a slave,
but God's child; and since you are his child,
God has made you also an heir"
(Galatians 4:7).

The New Testament use of the slave/
servant motif is interesting—one of those
beautiful biblical paradoxes. Accepting
salvation in Christ frees us from bondage
to sin (or, in a different sense, to the law),
while thrusting us into voluntary servi-
tude for the sake of our Lord, based solely
on our overflowing love and gratitude.

I appreciate the increments in the above
verse and elsewhere in terms of our status in God's sight. You and I, no longer slaves, have become willing servants
(though not spoken in this verse, we
know it from so many other references
to be true). From that point we make the
step to becoming sons and daughters.
And from there, in natural progression,
to heirs and heiresses. What a heady—
and amazing—succession!

February 25

Our Part

*"Do not conform to the pattern
of this world, but be transformed
by the renewing of your mind"
(Romans 12:2).*

"The opposite of bravery," suggests Robert Anthony, "is not cowardice but conformity." We all know the temptation to lose ourselves in a crowd. Adolescents, for all their brash shows of individuality, are eager to do just that. I find it comical to observe the predictability in their "nonconformity"; the unwritten strictures can be tightly drawn.

How attention-averse are you? Not in terms of distinction: we all crave that. But of the prospect of standing out for differences we fear might engender ridicule. Truth is, that brand of individuality is just as likely to win admiration. We've been transformed—and in the process drafted as Christ's recruits, accountable to assist in renewing the world. How likely is it for us to conform and transform at the same time?

February 26

Aging Love

"You have forsaken the love you had at first"
(Revelation 2:4).

There's something about observing youthful zeal that moves and convicts us. If there's one thing the young are not, it's complacent. Yet the edges of our love don't have to dull as we age. Because another thing the young are not is mellowed, and there's a strength in mature love that's hard to beat.

I enjoy witnessing older couples living in a softened, cultivated love. The kind that anticipates the other's response and inspires a knowing smile at the smallest gesture. The love that "gets" a joke at the same instant, even if it has lost some of its forward-looking idealism. The love that relishes the backward glance with the same titillation it felt when the moment was present tense. This serene devotion characterizes our love for God, too, as we mature in our faith. Far from forsaking the love we had at first, you and I can in the Spirit age our life of faith to "perfection."

February 27

Sure and Certain Hope

*". . . in the hope of eternal life,
which God, who does not lie, promised
before the beginning of time"
(Titus 1:2).*

We use the word *hope* rather broadly, but there's a world of difference between "I hope so" and "So let it be" (what we're declaring with each "Amen")—between random yearning and grounded anticipation. That first, open-ended kind of hope is in itself an incredible gift of God, a character trait that has seen countless people through the most desolate situations: years of languishing in prisons and concentration camps, under relentless oppression, and through devastating illness. There's a poignant quality in this kind of hope, admirable though it may be, because it teeters always on the verge of tragedy.

Hope in Christ, the hope of the resurrection, is different altogether. It too sees us through desperate times, but there's no uncertainty about the outcome. The question asked by this kind of hope is not *if?* but *when?* And that makes all the difference. On what does your hope rely?

Condition

*"If anyone obeys his word,
love for God is truly made complete
in them. This is how we know we are
in him: Whoever claims to live
in him must live as Jesus did"
(1 John 2:5–6).*

Poet Elizabeth Barrett Browning summons, "God's greatness flow around our incompleteness; Round our restlessness, his rest." In the process of enveloping us, God completes and heals, negating our inadequacies with his sufficiency. Living in him, we partake of the fullness of who he is.

As John makes clear, though, there's a condition that serves both as a requirement for and a confirmation of God's presence in our lives, and ours in his. Just in case we miss it the first time, John expresses it twice: "Whoever obeys his word" and "must live as Jesus did." Our hearts and wills must be compatible before our Lord will feel at home with, in, and around us.

February 29

Leaping Time

*"My heart leaps for joy, and with my song
I praise him" (Psalm 28:7).*

If you're reading this on a nonexistent
February 29, you're a particularly dedi-
cated devotional reader. I've chosen an
upbeat verse for today. The concept of
leaping serves for me as a springboard for
expressions of exuberance. I resonate with
this from Samuel Rutherford: "We may
sing beforehand, even in our winter storm
. . . no created powers can mar our Lord
Jesus' music, nor spill our song of joy."

Long about February 29 (or, better yet,
March 1), I'm emotionally prepped for
spring. The promise of rejuvenated life
in just three weeks (I'm a diehard literal-
ist about the coming of spring) inspires in
me thoughts of sprucing up. My eye turns
not only to my condo, garden, and ward-
robe but also to my attitude. The coming
of spring, not winter, is for me a time of
resolution. With what song do you praise
your Creator/Provider in springtime's
approach?

March

"It was one of those
March days when
the sun shines hot and the
wind blows cold:
when it is summer in the light,
and winter in the shade."

—Charles Dickens

March 1

Direction

"In their hearts humans plan their course, but the LORD establishes their steps"
(Proverbs 16:9).

I read the second clause in this verse as God's confirmation of a direction. God can establish my steps, remove roadblocks, and even provide a wind at my back to propel me along in the direction of his will. Alternatively, he may discourage my forward progress by making it difficult to buck his plan for me.

When we've set our hearts on a given course, we can construe God's dissuasion as a lack of love or interest. To the contrary, I recognize (in hindsight; I have particular situations in mind) that his willingness to encourage or discourage my steps is part of his gentle provision. My online thesaurus offers some surprising synonyms for *providence*, including *fate*, *chance*, *luck*, and *destiny*—all of which we as believers know to be direct opposites! Truth is, God manifests his infinite love for you and me by refusing to leave us directionless.

March 2

Memorization of the Heart

"The word is very near you;
it is in your mouth and in your
heart so you may obey it"
(Deuteronomy 30:14).

Memorization isn't internalization. The first is conscious, involving the mind, while the second is subconscious, involving the heart and will. Educators recognize this, resulting in emphases that are different from those of the past. In this information age, facts are fingertip ready. It's the applications that demand attention.

The same applies to the Law of God. When we approach his commands from interior motivation, we obey from the overflow of our love and gratitude. Jesus understood the importance of subconscious guiding principles, making it clear that "all the Law and the Prophets hang on . . . two commandments": to love God above all and our neighbor as ourselves. When we imprint a habitual course of action upon our psyche, our heart won't soon forget.

March 3

Lefties

"Among all these soldiers there were seven hundred select troops who were left-handed, each of whom could sling a stone at a hair and not miss"
(Judges 20:16).

The tribe of Benjamin cultivated left-handedness in select troops in a special ops force. The judge Ehud, we're told, used the element of surprise this ability afforded him in an assassination (Judges 3:15, 21).

For a long time we Westerners tried to force our lefties into the "right" mold. Why allow these misdirected folks to smudge their papers with an awkward pencil grip or upset the seating arrangement at a dining table? And how in the world do you teach them to knit? Ridiculous as this may seem, it's indicative of the value humans place on conformity. If you're a free spirit, celebrate your unconventionality. If not, at least make the attempt to appreciate that quality in others—remembering that God's Spirit is in the business of liberating our own!

March 4

Incremental Blessing

*"I will not drive [the Canaanites] out
in a single year, because the land would
become desolate and the wild animals
too numerous for you. Little by little
I will drive them out before you"*
(Exodus 23:29–30).

We serve a practical God, whose modus
operandi is usually to work within his own
natural laws. What would have happened
had God opted to wipe out the Canaanites
in one fell swoop in advance of the enter-
ing Israelites? This would have resolved a
lot of issues, but it would also have elimi-
nated valuable learning experiences, including the temptation for partial obedience
that would plague his reluctant people.

But making sure the land stayed populated
until the moment of handover served another critical purpose: preventing a prolif-
eration of wild animals that might have
proven more difficult to route than the
Canaanites. God's "reluctance" to act on
our every whim, to offer us what we want
when we want it, circumvents unantici-
pated grief for us too. When has God—little
by little—lifted obstacles from your way?

March 5

Your People

"'Go home to your own people and tell them how much the Lord has done for you'"
(Mark 5:19).

Sharing the good news doesn't have to be limited to strangers, acquaintances, coworkers, or friends. Unless our witness begins with and consistently includes those closest to us, it will remain artificial, forced, and insincere.

Some of the stories I most appreciate come from my eighty-five-year-old dad. Like a child I anticipate the outcomes, prepared to laugh or smile. And I love retelling (and more especially hearing Dad retell) those same stories to my daughters or granddaughter. It's the same with stories of the faith—not only those chronicled throughout God's Word but also (and at times especially) those that involve us personally. Have you shared with "your people" what God has done for you?

March 6

Ignorance . . . and Ignoring

*"My people are destroyed for lack
of knowledge" (Hosea 4:6).*

Under no jurisdiction is ignorance of the
law an excuse for breaking it. My tradition makes a distinction between God's
Word (special revelation) and his world
(general revelation). While it's possible to live in ignorance of his Word, the
signs of God's presence and activity in his
world can only be deliberately ignored.
Listen to Paul in Romans 1:20: "For since
the creation of the world God's invisible
qualities—his eternal power and divine
nature—have been clearly seen, being understood from what has been made, so
that people are without excuse."

Immanuel Kant cites the inklings of mo-
rality (a related issue) with which God
has endowed all humans: "Two things
fill the mind with ever new and increasing wonder and awe—the starry heavens
above me and the moral law within me."
What are you doing to combat ignorance,
and ignoring, in your life? In the lives of
others?

March 7

"Too Wonderful"

"God placed all things under his feet and appointed him to be head over everything for the church, which is his body, the fullness of him who fills everything in every way" (Ephesians 1:22–23).

"In whatever direction you turn, you will see God coming to meet you; nothing is void of him, he himself fills all his work." So observed Seneca the Younger, a Roman philosopher and contemporary of Jesus. Paul held a similar view of the ubiquitous presence of God. What a comfort to acknowledge that, wherever we are, he too is there.

Or does our comfort level depend on what we happen to be doing there? I recall my mom schooling the toddler me in the principle of God's all-seeing eyes. "You cannot hide from God," we sibs would sing, impressed by his prowess at Hide and Seek. David voices what sounds like a complaint in Psalm 139:5: "You hem me in behind and before" (verse 6). So his next words catch me by surprise: "Such knowledge is too wonderful for me." Our awareness of God's omnipresence can indeed be impossibly wonderful . . . provided we live consistently before him.

March 8

Red Flags

*"The sins of some are obvious, reaching
the place of judgment ahead of them;
the sins of others trail behind them"*
(1 Timothy 5:24).

The second half of this intriguing verse reminds me of those carefully concealed sins that tend to manifest themselves over time. On the extreme end, I picture a serial killer initially arrested for running a stop sign. How often aren't persons accused of serious crimes discovered to already be behind bars?

We're all sinners, but those of us who live by the Spirit (Romans 8:1–17) no longer live by or for sin. Those who "live according to the flesh," on the other hand, tend to conduct themselves by patterns of sin. This is an issue especially for the younger Christian, who might be subject to negative influences in friendship and dating relationships. Unless there is evidence of a radical conversion, what we see in someone else (once) is very often what we can expect to "get" from them again and again.

March 9

Distinctions

"Perhaps the reason he was separated from you for a little while was that you might have him back forever—no longer as a slave, but better than a slave, as a dear brother"
(Philemon 15–16).

Slavery in Paul's day wasn't the same as its recent Western iteration: a slave, though owned, was a part of a "household"; less than family, he or she was never treated as chattel. One similarity, though, was the eagerness of slaves to join the Christian Church. A reading of the short letter of Paul to Philemon snapshots the awkwardness this caused for those espousing the brotherhood and sisterhood of believers. Besides the issue of slavery, the early Church squabbled over the treatment of Jewish versus Gentile widows, the rich versus the poor at communion feasts, and the list goes on.

If there's one thing humans are good at—and Christians are hardly exempt—it's making distinctions. Which is a perfectly healthful ability, as long as is isn't applied to the valuation of people. Keeping in mind that the issue is one of worth, not role, what potentially unhealthy distinctions do you see in your church? In your heart?

March 10

A Matter of Quality

"What is mankind that you are mindful of them, human beings that you care for them?" (Psalm 8:4).

Fifty some years ago my mom read aloud to us kids a church library book about a Navajo family. An impressionable preschooler, I listened to one chapter with real consternation. Its title, five words expressed by little Lolita, caused me real consternation: "I wish I were a dog!" Understanding that the granting of this alarming wish would mark a giant step backward, I probed: "Why, Mumma? Why would Lolita wish for *that*?"

The four- or five-year-old me had no experience with the kind of pain that might cause people to decry their own humanity. But I did intuit the unbridgeable, qualitative gap between myself as a person—with a soul—and an animal. I understand better now the pain of life. But of one thing I'm sure: I'll never wish away my exalted, image-bearing status.

March 11

Beyond Ability

"I testify that they gave as much as they were able, and even beyond their ability"
(2 Corinthians 8:3).

Doing anything beyond our ability sounds like a contradiction, and humanly speaking that's true. But when we do something in and for the Lord, we aren't doing it humanly. As believers we live on borrowed strength, not in terms of its being temporary but in terms of its emanating from a source beyond (but still mysteriously within) ourselves.

Paul declares in Philippians 4:13 that he (and each of us by extension) can do "all this" (the 1984 NIV translation renders this "everything") through Christ, who is his strength. In what areas of your Christian life are you performing beyond your ability? In what areas is your Spirit-borrowed strength most apparent?

March 12

Living, Loving Hope

"Hope does not disappoint us"
(Romans 5:5 NIV 1984).

In a recent sermon on grief my pastor discussed the fact that we humans go on loving those who are gone. We may "hear" the trill of their laughter in a crowd or feel an inexplicable sense of their presence. This kind of ongoing love can be intensely meaningful for us as Christians.

I believe we can identify the operative ingredient here as hope. None of us knows what life in the renewed heavens and earth will be like. What we do know is that our deepest longings, beyond union with Christ, are for reunion with those "missing" ones our hearts still cherish. Beyond this, we know that the reality of our future state will be infinitely beyond the best we can imagine. If you find yourself loving a believer who is no longer at your side, rest in the assurance that your hope of reunion won't let you down.

March 13

Imagine . . .

*"God made the earth by his power;
he founded the world by his wisdom
and stretched out the heavens by his
understanding"* (Jeremiah 10:12).

Political correctness aside, I'm not above occasionally claiming the gender-based "prerogative" of changing my mind, usually with relatively minor impact. "That is the consolation of a little mind," quipped Frank Moore Colby; "you have the fun of changing it without impeding the progress of mankind."

In contrast, God's power and understanding are unlimited—as are his goodness and love. God's every action moves the created order in the direction of perfection and consummation. Can you imagine a situation in which any of those attributes—power, understanding, goodness, or love—were lacking in the Creator? Unthinkable? Not to the billions who don't believe. While you're imagining, try to consider the impact of disbelief on their quality of life. What a difference faith makes!

Meaningless!

*"Now all has been heard; here is the
conclusion of the matter: Fear God
and keep his commandments, for this
is the duty of all mankind"
(Ecclesiastes 12:13).*

The author of Ecclesiastes (likely Solomon) was on a systematic search for meaning, checking out and then rejecting first one thing and then another. The verse above states his conclusion.

Assuming that each of us will reach the same point, where do you stand on the continuum? To some degree this may depend on your age, on whether you've reached the summit of life's roller coaster or how far over the hill you've descended (or plummeted). What have you valued at one or another point in life? Wisdom, pleasure, work, advancement, wealth, diversity of investments, and youth all appear on the "Teacher's" list. To what do you ascribe ultimate value?

March 15

Apt and Timely

"A person finds joy in giving an apt reply—and how good is a timely word!"
(Proverbs 15:23).

Solomon wasn't talking about the quick-witted repartee we value in our improv-loving society. The apt reply and timely word don't have to be instantaneous or clever. In fact, a "pregnant" pause preceding our response can be appropriate and effective. Job's friends extended their pause to a full week of empathetic silence. Had what they said at that point been a little more apt, their timing might have been right on.

So much of what we say is calculated to make an impression, and that might give us some smug satisfaction—but probably not joy. There's one adjective in this verse, though, that we've overlooked: *good.* Saying the right thing, especially to a hurting person, for the purpose of doing them good is joy inducing. When has this been true for you? When have you been on the receiving end of such a word?

March 16

The Outcome

"We know that in all things God works for the good of those who love him, who have been called according to his purpose" *(Romans 8:28).*

"Faith," notes Collette Baron-Reid, "is believing that the outcome will be what it should be, no matter what it is." While that's a comforting statement, my theology allows me to agree only conditionally. From my Reformed perspective, Paul wasn't saying that every short-term outcome in life will be positive. God doesn't orchestrate every detail, even though his providence guards us continuously, and our well-being is close to his heart. Our circumstances often reflect personal choices, for good or ill. And God allows the devil limited sway in the affairs of life.

What Paul is referring to here is the final, overall outcome of our lives. He who has called us will be faithful to see us through. He'll refuse to let us go, no matter what adverse outcomes we may experience along the way. Now that's a source of comfort!

March 17

Shouldn't He Care . . . ?

"'And should I not have concern for the great city of Nineveh, in which there are more than a hundred and twenty thousand people who cannot tell their right hand from their left—and also many animals?'" (Jonah 4:11).

God's concern for that pagan city surprises me. But his mention of the animals there really takes me aback. This is far from being the only passage on this issue, one I'll admit to having brushed aside for most of my life.

Just what is God's relationship to and design for the animal realm? Isaiah speaks of wolves lying with lambs, but what do we make of such imagery? My conception of ultimate reality, uninformed as it is (the Bible is tantalizingly tacit on detail), is becoming more expansive. Will there be animals on the new earth? I can't help but think so, given God's obvious delight in this aspect of creation and the close ties many people have established with them. The same animals we've known and loved? Someday we'll know. Are you someone who's longing to find out?

March 18

Preserving God's Reputation

*"Then the nations will know that
I am the L*ORD*, declares the Sovereign L*ORD*,
when I am proved holy through you before
their eyes" (Ezekiel 36:23).*

Have you ever thought of God's holiness
being demonstrated through you? The
opposite is too often true: the world is
quick to judge God by us, especially when
a negative conclusion of hypocrisy (or
worse) allows people to ease themselves
off the hook for their sinful behavior.

Has a scandal within the Christian com-
munity caused you to cringe, not for yourself but for the reputation of your Lord?
Do you hurt when Christians deny him,
betray him, or otherwise malign his name?
The devil works hard among believers, but
we are also uniquely equipped to deal with
his onslaughts. If you and I can each con-
vict one person of God's holiness, think of
the eternal difference that will make!

March 19

Prime Time

"At just the right time, when we were still powerless, Christ died for the ungodly"
(Romans 5:6).

What was there in particular that made the time prime for Jesus' birth, ministry, death, and resurrection? From a social/geographic/political standpoint, of course, several factors (like common language, excellent roads, and the *Pax Romana* [peace of Rome]) were conducive to the birth of the Church and the spread of the gospel.

Beyond that, we can only concede the impeccable timing of the Author of time, the particulars of which are beyond our need to know. We hear confirmation from Jesus' own lips in John 17:1 that the hour set by the Father for commencement of the final events leading up to the crucifixion had come. What a comfort to know that, at precisely the right moment, that same Christ will return for us in glory! Our role? Simply to be ready.

March 20

Easter Roses

"I am a rose of Sharon, a lily of the valleys"
(Song of Songs 2:1).

My daughter's manager is an expatriate from the Middle East, a Christian who understands religious persecution first-hand. This man enjoys Christian holidays in a special way, reveling in all things Christmas and Easter. A flower lover, he asked her to purchase for the hotel some "Easter roses." She chuckled at the form of this request for lilies; in this man's mind a flower by any other name would still be a rose.

I love these lines from the classic carol "Lo, How a Rose E'er Blooming": "It came, a floweret bright, amid the cold of winter, when half spent was the night." With the Advent of Easter the morning dawned, and the white lily now connotes purity, life, and renewal. Still, I like the analogy of an Easter rose. For we still worship the same floweret bright, now in the effulgence of his Easter glory.

March 21

Changing Seasons

*"'Praise be to the name of God for ever
and ever; wisdom and power are his.
He changes times and seasons"
(Daniel 2:20–21).*

The changing of the seasons—which
comes to my mind on this first full day
of spring—reminds me of God's wisdom
and power. The cycle of the year holds
different associations for us as individuals, depending upon our experiences, dis-
positions, times of life, and geographical
locations.

I grew up in Southern California before
coming to Michigan decades ago to at-
tend my denominational college. But
those delightful seasonal changes are a
large part of what has kept me here. I'm
hooked on seasons—and on the way they
define and punctuate my life. They remind me of a Creator who is both eter-
nally faithful and endlessly, dynamically
energetic and imaginative.

March 22

The Illusion

"I hope that, as you have understood us in part, you will come to understand fully"
(2 Corinthians 1:13–14).

The letters of 1 and 2 Corinthians were difficult for Paul to write; he was addressing crippling conflict within this church, was disappointed by the news, and understood the risk that his long-distance communication might not be fully understood or accepted in the spirit he intended. Particularly with regard to communication attempts not substantiated by visual cues or body language, that kind of risk is always real.

"The single biggest problem in communication," noted George Bernard Shaw, "is the illusion that it has taken place." What extra steps can you take, particularly when it comes to your interactions on spiritual or other sensitive or significant areas, to verify understanding? When perception is critical, it's best to take nothing for granted.

March 23

Bad Versus Worst?

"Why are you silent while the wicked swallow up those more righteous than themselves?" (Habakkuk 1:13).

Habakkuk, the complaining prophet, was well aware of Judah's sin but used a common ploy in his argument with God: pitting the notorious wickedness of the Babylonians against the "second-degree" impiety of God's people. "Why, God," he rationalized in so many words, "do you allow the worst to swallow up the merely bad?"

This kind of bad-worse-worst evaluation has appealed to believers throughout history. But it misses the point of self-examination and repentance. Beyond the truth that only God is qualified to judge the heart, we do well to acknowledge our own vulnerability: "Watch yourselves, or you also may be tempted" (Galatians 6:1), and "If you think you are standing firm, be careful that you don't fall!" (1 Corinthians 10:12). Those are timely reminders for all of us.

March 24

Ready?

"'Believe in the light while you have the light, so that you may become children of light'" (John 12:36).

Jesus was preparing his disciples for his coming death. In the next verse John goes on to comment that Jesus left and hid himself from his disciples. Was he in some small way preparing them for his leave-taking?

I chuckle at George Carlin's "Weather forecast for tonight: dark." That's only provisionally true, of course (Jesus has risen and ascended, and the Spirit disseminates light in and through us). But how ready are we for the full radiance to come? Frederick Buechner addressed this issue movingly: "People are prepared for everything except for the fact that beyond the darkness of their blindness there is a great light. They are prepared for a mustard-seed kingdom of God no bigger than the eye of a newt but not for the great banyan it becomes with birds in its branches singing Mozart. They are prepared for the potluck supper at First Presbyterian but not for the marriage supper of the lamb." To what degree are you anticipating Christ's light?

Evangelists

*"Do your best to present yourself
to God as one approved, a worker who
does not need to be ashamed and
who correctly handles the word of truth"
(2 Timothy 2:15).*

Correctly handling the Word requires care. It isn't that it's fragile: if anything we encounter in our earthly lives can stand on its own, it's God's divine revelation of himself to the world.

Our job as ambassadors of that Word is to faithfully represent its Author and his truth. While I was editor in the Bible department of a large Christian publishing house, employees were at times asked to be "evangelists" for certain products or programs. The job of an evangelist is to whet appetites, to uphold the author's reputation, and to promote the theme in clear and unambiguous terms, always remaining true to the writer's character and purpose. How well are you promoting the words of life from the Author of life?

March 26

Our Element

"This grace was given us in Christ Jesus before the beginning of time"
(2 Timothy 1:9).

Time, like oxygen—they're both elements in which we experience physical existence—is from God's side a temporary concession to accommodate our limitations. But Douglas Horton declares that "on Easter Day the veil between time and eternity thins to gossamer." That's the day Christ sloughed off the constraints that had prevented us from attaining our full spiritual element as God's people.

Eternity isn't some nebulous future prospect. Jesus' resurrection ushered us into the early inklings of a glorious forever, removing the barrier that had restricted our entree into the Father's presence. In the words of poet Ralph Waldo Emerson, Christ "takes men out of time and makes them feel eternity." And once time has run its course, eternity's glory will be everything.

March 27

God's Best

"'You asked, "Who is this that obscures my plans without knowledge?" Surely I spoke of things I did not understand, things too wonderful for me to know'" (Job 42:3).

If springtime isn't becoming evident by this point in March (which is often the case in West Michigan), I start to chafe in something irrationally close to anger. Come on, come on! I seethe internally. Enough winter already!

I do a lot better at accepting big disappointments—like the loss of my job five years ago, followed two months later by the loss of contact with three grandchildren— than I do those niggling frustrations. It can be surprisingly easy to identify God's hand in the big stuff, whether personal, larger scale, or even global. But how readily do we accept his jurisdiction over all things, including the weather? Whether this day brings me a crocus or a cross is within God's discretion. Either way, it will be, in the words of a beloved old song, "what he deems best."

March 28

The Extra in the Ordinary

"'Greater love has no one than this:
to lay down one's life for one's friends'"
(John 15:13).

A caution from Mother Teresa gives me
pause: "Don't think that love, to be true,
has to be extraordinary." While I believe
that Christ-motivated love is by its nature distinctive, not every word or deed it
engenders will be noteworthy. Not every
contact of Jesus was remarkable either.

I want to avoid reading anything into
Jesus' words, above. He said, and meant,
to die on behalf of others. But it is certainly possible for Christ-followers to
"give" themselves to his cause in such
a way that the amalgam of a lifetime of
ordinary love becomes decidedly extra.
If you and I are willing, as consistently
as possible, to represent our Lord through
lives of love, the effect of our service will
be exceptional. When we're faithful, we
can count on the Spirit to add his extra—
that kingdom *oomph!*—to our ordinary.

March 29

God with Us?

*"'How will anyone know that you
are pleased with me and with your
people unless you go with us?'"
(Exodus 33:16).*

The United States isn't God's chosen land
or people. Certainly not in the way an-
cient Israel was. Nationalism based on the
notion of God walking with a nation, especially into battle, is a dangerous game
to play. Still, the declaration that "In
God We Trust" causes the world to look
on with expectation or derision. Our na-
tional sins can be a little like exhibiting
road rage while driving with an ichthus
(fish) symbol on our bumper.

Still, it's legitimate and necessary for us as
believing citizens to adopt a stance of hu-
mility and repentance, beseeching God to
heal our land (see 2 Chronicles 7:14). The
Lord honors those who take him and his
words seriously.

March 30

The Open-Ended Question

"'What things?' he asked"
(Luke 24:19).

The Emmaus wayfarers were incredulous that Jesus could have been in Jerusalem without knowing the events that had transpired there. What restraint it must have taken for Jesus to respond with an open-ended question of his own. And how different the encounter would have been had he chosen instead to overawe them with the whole truth.

Jesus' modus operandi was never to blow people away. Such an approach would have negated his relational effectiveness in any given situation. It's the same for us today. When we approach our Lord, overwhelmed by trouble, he prods us gently with "What things?" forcing us to slow down long enough to define and articulate what's on our mind and heart. Isn't it often our perspective on a situation—not the situation itself—that needs to change?

March 31

Outpouring

*"He poured out his life
unto death, and was numbered
with the transgressors"
(Isaiah 53:12).*

I'm moved by the image of Jesus pouring out his life. On the one hand I visualize an outflow of lifeblood—a poignant, passive image, a being poured out. Yet on a deeper level I see spilling over a love too thrusting to be contained—the definition of proactivity, a voluntary pouring out. Yes, Jesus obeyed the Father, but the decision to sacrifice himself was his own.

The only appropriate response to such love will be voluntary and insistent too. When have you experienced a love so overwhelming you could neither squelch it nor hold it in? A gratitude so urgent you just had to pass it on? That's the impetus of the Christian faith, an unstoppable momentum to spread an unquenchable love.

acknowledgments

Title Page

Yoko Ono: http://www.gardendigest.com/time.htm#Quotes

Winter

Andrew Wyeth: http://www.gardendigest.com/winter.htm

January

Patricia Hampl: http://www.gardendigest.com/monjan.htm

January 1

Charles Lamb: http://www.quotegarden.com/new-year.html

January 7

Jeannette Winterson: http://thinkexist.com/quotes/with/keyword/snowflake/

January 10

Adrienne Ivey: http://www.livinglifefully.com/winter.htm

January 14

Madeleine L'Engle: http://www.tentmaker.org/Quotes/faithquotes.htm

January 16

James F. Byrnes: http://www.quotationspage.com/subjects/security/

January 21

Abraham Joshua Heschel: http://www.wisdomquotes.com/topics/humanity/

January 22

Ruth Stout: http://www.quotegarden.com/winter.html

January 23

Margaret Atwood: http://www.quotegarden.com/valentine.html

January 24

William Safire: http://www.finestquotes.com/select_quote-category-Grammar-page-0.htm

January 30

Margaret Fairless Barger: http://www.finestquotes.com/select_quote-category-Nostalgia-page-0.htm

January 31

Henry Wadsworth Longfellow: http://thinkexist.com/quotes/with/keyword/cold/

February

Jean Paul Richter: http://www.specialty-calendars.com/winter.html

February 1

Franklin Thomas: http://www.quotegarden.com/black-history.html

February 2

Jeremy Taylor: http://www.quotegarden.com/life.html

February 3

Eleanor Roosevelt: http://www.wisdomquotes.com/topics/conscience/index2.html

February 4

Antoine de Saint-Exupéry: http://www.quotegarden.com/trees.html

February 5

Martin Luther King Jr.: http://www.wisdomquotes.com/topics/conflict/index2.html

February 6

George Lancaster Spalding: http://www.quotegarden.com/faith.html

February 7

African proverb: http://www.finestquotes.com/select_quote-category-Sadness-page-1.htm

February 8

George Chapman: http://www.brainyquote.com/quotes/keywords/cold_3.html

February 10

Beverly Sills: http://thinkexist.com/quotations/glory/3.htm

February 13

Emily Dickinson: http://www.quotegarden.com/heartache.html

February 15

Gail Barison: http://www.gardendigest.com/monfeb.htm

February 17

Friedrich Nietzsche: http://thinkexist.com/quotations/trust/

February 18

William Cullen Bryant: http://www.gardendigest.com/monfeb.htm

February 19

William Shakespeare: http://thinkexist.com/quotations/glory/

February 21

William Sharp: http://www.gardendigest.com/monfeb.htm

February 22

Billy Graham: http://thinkexist.com/quotes/with/keyword/storms/

February 23

Unknown author: http://thinkexist.com/quotes/with/keyword/discouragement/

February 25

Robert Anthony: http://quotationsbook.com/quotes/tag/conformity/

February 28

Elizabeth Barrett Browning: http://www.alwaysbesideme.com/quotes-about-god.html

February 29

Samuel Rutherford: http://dailychristianquote.com/dcqjoy.html

March

Charles Dickens : http://www.gardendigest.com/monmar.htm

March 6

Immanuel Kant: http://www.wisdomquotes.com/topics/conscience/

March 7

Seneca the Younger: http://www.alwaysbesideme.com/quotes-about-god.html

March 13

Frank Moore Colby: http://www.brainyquote.com/quotes/keywords/consolation.html

March 16

Collette Baron-Reid: http://www.quotegarden.com/faith.html

March 22

George Bernard Shaw: http://thinkexist.com/quotations/communication/

March 24

George Carlin: http://www.quotegarden.com/weather.html

Frederick Buechner: http://dailychristianquote.com/dcqjoy2.html

March 26

Douglas Horton: http://christianstoriesonline.com/easter_quotes.html

Ralph Waldo Emerson: http://www.holidays-easter.net/easter-quotes/
easter-bible-quotes/168-he-takes-men-out-of-time-and-makes-them-feel-
eternity.html

March 28

Mother Teresa: http://anglicanprayer.wordpress.com/category/
church-seasons/advent/advent-quotes/

www.ingramcontent.com/pod-product-compliance
Lightning Source LLC
Chambersburg PA
CBHW072239290326
41934CB00008BB/1355